DISASTER!

Mary McIntosh

Oxford Bookworms
Factfiles

OXFORD UNIVERSITY PRESS

OXFORD
UNIVERSITY PRESS

Great Clarendon Street, Oxford OX2 6DP

Oxford University Press is a department of the University of Oxford.
It furthers the University's objective of excellence in research, scholarship,
and education by publishing worldwide in

Oxford New York

Auckland Cape Town Dar es Salaam Hong Kong Karachi
Kuala Lumpur Madrid Melbourne Mexico City Nairobi
New Delhi Shanghai Taipei Toronto

With offices in

Argentina Austria Brazil Chile Czech Republic France Greece
Guatemala Hungary Italy Japan Poland Portugal Singapore
South Korea Switzerland Thailand Turkey Ukraine Vietnam

OXFORD and OXFORD ENGLISH are registered trade marks of
Oxford University Press in the UK and in certain other countries

© Oxford University Press 1998

The moral rights of the author have been asserted

Database right Oxford University Press (maker)

First published 1998

2010 2009 2008 2007 2006

10 9 8 7 6 5

No unauthorized photocopying

All rights reserved. No part of this publication may be reproduced,
stored in a retrieval system, or transmitted, in any form or by any means,
without the prior permission in writing of Oxford University Press,
or as expressly permitted by law, or under terms agreed with the
appropriate reprographics rights organization. Enquiries concerning
reproduction outside the scope of the above should be sent to the
ELT Rights Department, Oxford University Press, at the address above

You must not circulate this book in any other binding or cover
and you must impose this same condition on any acquirer

Any websites referred to in this publication are in the public
domain and their addresses are provided by Oxford University Press
for information only. Oxford University Press disclaims any
responsibility for the content

ISBN-13: 978 0 19 422851 0
ISBN-10: 0 19 422851 7

Printed in Hong Kong

Oxford Bookworms Factfiles

Original readers giving varied and interesting information
about a range of non-fiction topics. Language is carefully
graded for elementary to intermediate students at *Oxford
Bookworms* Stages 1–4. *Factfiles* develop overall reading
comprehension and train students to scan texts for specific
information. A variety of after reading activities
encourages students to work actively with the text.

OXFORD BOOKWORMS

For a full list of titles in all the Oxford Bookworms series,
please refer to the Oxford English catalogue.

Oxford Bookworms Starters

Original fiction for students starting to read in English.
Stories are carefully graded and supported by clear, high-
quality illustrations.

The Oxford Bookworms Library

A wide range of original and adapted stories, both classic
and modern, which take learners from elementary to
advanced level through six carefully graded language
stages.

Oxford Bookworms Playscripts

A range of plays, designed both for reading and performing
in the classroom.

The Oxford Bookworms Collection

Fiction by well-known classic and modern authors. Texts
are not abridged or simplified in any way.

ACKNOWLEDGEMENTS

The publishers would like to thank the following for permission to reproduce photographs: Bridgeman Art Library pp. 6 (Guildhall
Library, Corporation of London), 7; Bruce Coleman p 37 (J Foott Productions); Corbis-Bettmann-Reuter pp. 39 (crane), 41; e.t. archive
pp. 3 (dog/National Archaeological Museum Naples),9 (bucket and helmet/Museum of London); Geoscience Features Picture Library p
1; Imax Corporation p 13 (Undersea Imaging International); Museum of London p 8; NASA pp. 31, 32 (close-up); Popperfoto pp. 16, 17,
19 (Reuter), 23; Rex Features pp. 10 (C. Sachs/Sipa), 34 (G. Orth/Sipa); Science Photo Library pp. 29 (A. Tsiaras), 36 (clean-up/V. Vick);
Spectrum Colour Library p 2 (J. Gladwin); Frank Spooner Pictures pp. 3 (musicians/Figaro Magazine), 5 (E. Bouvet), 25 (Bartholomew),
27 (Shone), 30 (M. Brown), 32 (watching/M. Brown), 36 (bird/A. Dail), 39 (building/H. Chip); Sygma pp. 18 (M. Philippot), 21
(bank/Keystone), 21 (helicopter/Manchete), 24 (Baldev), 38 (Hashimoto); Topham Picturepoint pp. 4, 15 (Associated Press); Ulster Folk &
Transport Museum p 11 (Harland & Wolff Collection HI548)

1 Introduction

For thousands of years, people have been interested in disasters. We are both excited and frightened by disasters, and in our modern world, they help to sell newspapers and fill the news we see on television.

Disasters bring out the best and the worst in people's characters. We hear and read stories of great bravery, as well as stories of selfishness. Perhaps it is only in a disaster that a person's true character appears.

The disasters in this book make us think and ask many different questions. Firstly, what causes disasters? Sometimes, we can see that a human mistake caused a disaster, like the Great Fire of London, and the Bhopal disaster in India. When many people die of hunger, there is usually a political or economic cause for the disaster. Other great disasters, like tornadoes, volcanoes and earthquakes, have been caused by the forces of nature, and we cannot do much to prevent them.

The same mistakes will probably not be made twice, but can we learn from past disasters? We must certainly hope that scientists have learnt from the Chernobyl nuclear disaster, and from the *Challenger* space shuttle disaster.

Are there ways in which future disasters can be prevented? The Japanese people have certainly become good at preparing for earthquakes, and as a result, many lives have probably been saved. Computers and many scientific machines can help to give us warnings of possible disasters.

However, it is probably true to say that we shall never completely control the forces of nature. And although science and computers help us in so many ways, we can never completely prevent human mistakes.

Vesuvius today

2 The Volcano Vesuvius

One million people now live and work in the crowded, noisy city of Naples in Italy. Few of them lift their eyes to look up at the great volcano, Vesuvius, which rises, nearly 1,300 metres high, to the east of the city.

In the year A.D.79, nearly 2,000 years ago, the people of the busy town of Pompeii hurried about their lives without thinking of Vesuvius. Pompeii is twenty kilometres south-east of Naples, and it is only ten kilometres from the great volcano. At that time, Pompeii was a rich town of 20,000 people with a busy port and market. All around the town were the beautiful homes of rich merchants and their families.

Disaster!

Then, on 24th August, A.D.79, everything changed for ever. In the middle of the morning, the earth began to shake; cups fell off tables, and holes appeared in the ground. People remembered the disastrous earthquake that had hit the town seventeen years before. Was this the beginning of another earthquake?

Dogs started to bark, birds flew away, and a strange silence seemed to hang over the town. At midday, a great cloud of ash rose up out of Vesuvius and into the air. That afternoon, with a terrible noise a thousand times louder than thunder, the top of the volcano was blown twenty kilometres into the air, and sheets of flame lit up the darkened sky. Vesuvius was erupting!

A south-east wind quickly blew the cloud of ash towards the town of Pompeii. People panicked and tried to escape. But for many, it was too late. In two days, the town was covered in four metres of ash and stones. About two thousand people were killed by the cloud of hot gases and ash. Others were buried in hot mud and stones.

The small port of Herculaneum, which lies between Vesuvius and the sea, met a more violent death. After the first eruption of Vesuvius, many people of Herculaneum had left the town. Those who remained thought that they were safe, because the winds did not take the ash and smoke in their direction.

■ The cloud of ash from the eruption of Vesuvius in A.D.79 crossed the Mediterranean Sea and reached North Africa.

■ When the island of Krakatau in Indonesia erupted in 1883, people in Australia heard it 4,800 kilometres away! About 36,000 people lost their lives, and only three small parts of the island remained. Then in 1927, a new island appeared. It was called Anak Krakatau, which means 'child of Krakatau'.

Mosaics in Pompeii. They are made of many little stones.

- On 18 May 1980, Mount St. Helens in Washington State, USA, blew its top. The top 400 metres of the mountain were blown eighteen kilometres into the sky, and a cloud of ash and gas followed.

- Vesuvius has erupted more than seventy times since A.D. 79. It erupts approximately once every twenty-seven years. The last eruption was in 1944.

However, on 25th August, the day after the first eruption, Herculaneum was suddenly covered by a violent river of hot ash and mud. In a few hours, the town was buried under twenty metres of hardened rock from the volcano.

In some ways, this eruption of Vesuvius was just like any other disaster caused by volcanoes. People died miserable deaths, and the families and survivors had to learn to make new lives for themselves. So why do we remember this eruption of Vesuvius as something special? Let us consider how we have come to know about life in Italy at that time.

In A.D. 79, Pompeii and Herculaneum were controlled by the great city of Rome. We know much about Rome and its people, through books written in the Latin

Herculaneum

- In November 1985, the Nevado del Ruiz volcano in Colombia erupted. The eruption was small, but it caused a river of mud, which covered the city of Armero. More than 20,000 people lost their lives.

Disaster!

language. Virgil and Pliny were famous writers of that time. In fact, there were two writers named Pliny. Pliny the elder was killed during the eruption of Vesuvius. He was the uncle of Pliny the younger, who survived and wrote a detailed description of the disaster.

However, in order to learn more about the world of the Romans at that time, we need more than books. We need things like plates, cups, coins, rings, bracelets and buildings.

The eruption of Vesuvius killed people suddenly, in the middle of a very ordinary day. Then the mud covered their bodies, which stayed untouched for many centuries. This had a surprising result: today, Pompeii and Herculaneum show us the everyday life of these two Roman towns nearly two thousand years ago.

In the remains of Pompeii and Herculaneum, archaeologists have discovered the houses and streets of the two towns: the shops, the street-signs, paintings and mosaics. They have also found the theatres, the bars, the kitchens, and the town baths. From these places, and from the things found there, many interesting facts have been discovered about life in Roman times. For example, in the open-air theatre of Pompeii, the bones of dead gladiators have been discovered. Gladiators fought animals and each other – and often died – while crowds of people watched and enjoyed themselves.

Archaeologists have also found graffiti – writing on the walls – which tell us what ordinary people were feeling and thinking, just as graffiti do today. Perhaps the people of Roman times were really quite similar to us today!

So the disaster which hit the people of Pompeii and Herculaneum in A.D.79 has given us a very real and meaningful lesson in the history of Italy and the Roman people.

■ Lake Nyos lies at the top of a volcano in Cameroon, West Africa. In August 1986, a strange gas rose up from the lake. It made a cloud over all the villages nearby, killing more than 1,200 people.

Nyos after the gas cloud

■ In 1963, a volcano erupted under the sea, and so the new island of Surtsey appeared, thirty-two kilometres south-west of Iceland! Now Surtsey is more than 2.5 kilometres across, and many plants, insects and birds live there.

3 The Great Fire of London

In the seventeenth century, London was a city full of rats. Rats in the streets, rats in the houses, rats in the shops. The rats brought dirt and disease to the people. In the year 1665, thousands of people in London died from a terrible disease carried by rats. Nobody felt safe from disease and death.

The next year, 1666, there was a long hot summer. People were glad to enjoy the sunshine, and they felt that it probably helped the city to get rid of disease.

But in fact the disease was finally destroyed by something much more powerful: fire.

■ Before the fire, there had been many wooden houses and shops on London Bridge, but they were all destroyed.

London before the Fire

Disaster!

It was two o'clock in the morning on Monday, 2nd September 1666. John Farynor, the King's baker, lived above his baker's shop, near the River Thames and London Bridge. Mr. Farynor was asleep, but it was time for his men to start baking bread for the King's breakfast. King Charles II liked fresh bread in the morning.

One of Mr. Farynor's men woke up and went to light the kitchen fires. Mr. Farynor kept a lot of wood in his kitchen, ready to bake the bread every day.

That morning, the man discovered that some wood had caught fire, and the kitchen was beginning to burn!

Quickly, the man woke Mr. Farynor and shouted 'Fire! Fire!' Soon the whole house was awake, and people were running everywhere, trying to escape. Mr. Farynor escaped by climbing on to the roof of his house and jumping on to the roof of the next house. One woman was not so lucky. She stayed in the house, perhaps hoping to save some of her money or her valuables. She burned to death.

■ The Monument is a tall, thin tower which you can still see in London today. It was built in 1671, near Pudding Lane where the Great Fire started. The Monument has 345 steps leading from the bottom to the top.

The Great Fire of London

Disaster!

- Samuel Pepys (1633–1703) wrote a description of the Great Fire of London in his diary. He wrote his diary in a special code, which nobody understood until John Smith worked out how to read it in 1825.

- In 1666, 460,000 people lived in London. It was a busy, exciting city. Ships from London sailed to America, India, China, and many other parts of the world.

- Twenty-four hours after the fire was controlled, nobody could walk on the streets without shoes – the ground was still too hot.

After the fire had started, a strong wind blew the flames towards the west. More and more people panicked, and they all tried to save their valuables.

The fire moved quickly through the old city. The houses were made of wood, and were built very close together in narrow streets. As the fire moved, it destroyed everything in its way. It could not cross the River Thames, but it did reach the buildings beside the river. Ships from many foreign countries stopped here to leave their strange and exciting cargoes. Soon London was smelling of hot peppers and burning brandy! And hot metal was flowing like a river through the streets!

Sir Thomas Bludworth, the Lord Mayor of London, thought that the fire could be put out easily. Later, he tried to organize the fire-fighting, but he gave up the job. It was then that the King and his brother took control of the fire.

King Charles soon realized that the fire was completely out of control. He called a meeting of the Privy Council – a group of his special advisers. Together, they decided to make several 'fire posts' in the city, where the fire-fighters were given everything they needed to fight the fire. King Charles led the fight, and he gave a guinea coin to every helper. (One guinea was worth a bit more than one English pound, which was a lot of money in those days.) He worked for thirty hours without sleep, and he was much loved for his bravery.

A water pump

Disaster!

King Charles and his men decided to clear part of the city by pulling down some houses, so that the fire would have nothing to burn there. This 'fire break' stopped the fire, and by Wednesday, 5th September, it was finally under control.

We have some very good descriptions of the fire that night. Samuel Pepys was an important man in the government of King Charles, and every day he wrote a diary about his life in London at that time. He wrote that one of the women in his house, Jane, 'called us up about three in the morning, to tell us of a great fire in the City. So I rose ... and went to her window ... I thought it far enough off, and so went to bed again to sleep.'

By the time Pepys woke up again, the fire had already burnt three hundred houses in London. He went to King Charles to tell him that the fire was really serious.

The Great Fire of London had several important results. It finally stopped the disease which had killed so many people in 1665. It destroyed eighty-seven churches and about 13,000 wooden houses. The houses were neither safe nor healthy. After the Great Fire, more houses were built of stone or brick, so London became a cleaner and more healthy city.

The Great Fire also destroyed the old St. Paul's Cathedral, so King Charles asked Sir Christopher Wren to plan a new cathedral. In 1675, Sir Christopher finally began the 'new' St. Paul's Cathedral, which still stands in London today.

- More than three-quarters of London burnt down during the fire, but only a few people died.

- The building of the new St. Paul's Cathedral cost £736,952.

A fire-fighter's bucket

A fire-fighter's helmet

4 The *Titanic*

'Unsinkable!' 'The safest ship in the world!' 'A palace on water!'

Those were some of the words used to describe the *Titanic* before she sailed on her first journey, from Southampton in England to New York in the USA on 10th April 1912. She had more than 2,220 people on board.

The *Titanic* was indeed a special ship. Her rich, first-class passengers enjoyed more luxuries than on almost any other ship before. The furniture and the rooms were like those in a palace. There were libraries, restaurants, dining rooms, reading rooms and a swimming pool on board. And the ship was one of the first to have radio, which was used by Captain Edward Smith and his sailors to keep in contact with land and with other ships. Radio was also used by rich passengers to send messages to their friends!

■ The film *Titanic* is one of the most successful films ever. It creates the atmosphere of the ship and its voyage, but much of the story is not true.

The Titanic *leaves Southampton*

Disaster!

However, not all the *Titanic*'s passengers were rich. Many second-class and third-class passengers were hoping to start a new, better life in the USA. The third-class passengers had very small rooms deep down in the ship, and they did not enjoy any of the luxuries for which the Titanic was so famous.

On Sunday, 14th April, after five days at sea, the *Titanic* was 153 kilometres south of Newfoundland in the north Atlantic. Although it was spring-time, Captain Smith knew that there might be ice in the sea. But he was confident that ice was not a real danger. After all, the *Titanic* was unsinkable!

As it was Sunday, the passengers and sailors went to church in the morning, then they returned to their normal daily routines. Men played cards, ladies laughed and talked, while they enjoyed beautiful music. Rich passengers sent radio messages to their friends in New York and London. Captain Smith was invited to a dinner party.

■ The Titanic was sailing at a time of strong class differences in Europe and America. Several life-boats were not completely filled at first, because the first-class passengers did not want to share a life-boat with second- or third-class passengers.

On board the Titanic

Disaster!

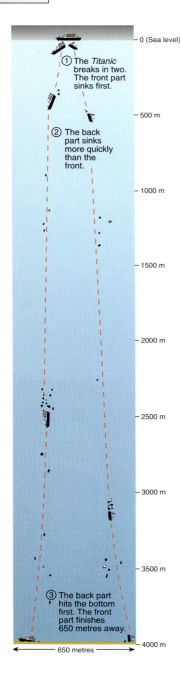

During that cold evening, the *Titanic* received seven radio messages warning of the danger of ice. The Captain was aware of at least one warning, but he ordered the ship to continue straight towards New York. After all, the *Titanic* was unsinkable.

Later that night, the look-out boy saw an iceberg – a great piece of ice in the sea. He rang the alarm bell immediately, and at last the Captain and crew took the warning of ice seriously. The Captain desperately tried to change the direction of the ship, away from danger. Too late! The *Titanic* was 268 metres long, 32 metres high, and it weighed over 60,000 tonnes. It could not change direction quickly.

A few minutes before midnight, the unsinkable *Titanic* hit the iceberg, which made a hole 90 metres long in the ship's side. When the Captain went to see the hole and saw water entering the ship, he immediately ordered the lifeboats – although he knew that there were only enough lifeboats to save just over half the people on board.

There was so much music and noise on board the *Titanic*, the passengers did not at first notice that the engines were strangely silent. It was half an hour before the first-class passengers realized that anything had happened. The sailors went down the stairs to warn the poorer passengers, who then desperately tried to find their way up to the lifeboats. For some, the long journey up through the ship took more than one hour.

When the lifeboats were ready, women and children were ordered to get in first. Many families were separated, and many children never saw their fathers again.

Edith Brown, aged fifteen, was with her rich parents who had decided to start a new life in the USA. Before the journey, her father had had a bad dream about the idea, but her mother had decided that they must go.

Disaster!

Mr. Brown's face was white as he boarded the *Titanic* at Southampton, and again he looked white when he entered the family's rooms that cold night, saying, 'You'd better put on your life-jackets and something warm. It's cold on deck ... We've struck an iceberg ...' In their cabin the family left all their valuables. Edith and her mother escaped to a life-boat, but she never saw her beloved father again.

From her lifeboat, Edith Brown saw one end of the ship sink into the freezing water. Suddenly, all the lights went out, and where there had been laughter and light, there were suddenly screams and darkness.

As the sun rose the next morning, Edith, her mother, and the other survivors saw a sea full of bodies and icebergs. She and her mother were picked up by the *Carpathia*, the ship that received the *Titanic*'s calls for help. In the early hours of 15th April, the *Carpathia* saved 705 people from the sinking *Titanic*.

Edith Brown's experience of the *Titanic* disaster had changed her life and her character for ever. One very

- The wreck of the *Titanic* was finally discovered in September 1985. In the following years, US and French teams took photos of the wreck deep under the sea, and they brought up money and other valuables. In 1996, a tourist ship visited the site of the *Titanic*.

- Millvina Dean, who lost her father in the disaster, was the youngest survivor of the Titanic. She was six weeks old when it sank, but she is proud to have three paintings of the Titanic on the walls of her house.

The Titanic *today*

Disaster!

■ The *Titanic* sank on 15 April 1912. Several of the survivors have died on 15 April – many more than we would normally expect. It seems that the painful experiences make death on that date more probable.

good thing happened to her. As a result of the *Titanic* disaster, she met her husband, Fred, to whom she was happily married for sixty years. Together they had ten children, and many grandchildren and great-grandchildren. She died in 1997, aged one hundred.

Many other survivors never got over their experience of the disaster. Lilian Asplund was travelling with her parents, her twin brother, and three other brothers. They were in third class, where only twenty-three out of seventy-six children survived. When they reached the top deck, most of the lifeboats were full, so the family decided that they would die together. However, a sailor separated them and threw Lilian and her smallest brother into a life-boat. Lilian's father pushed his wife in with them. Then another man jumped on top of Lilian's mother, and the life-boat was lowered into the water. When Lilian's mother finally looked up, she only saw Lilian and her little brother. She never saw the rest of the family again.

Lilian, her little brother and her mother stayed together for the rest of their lives. Her mother died on 15th April 1964, the fiftieth anniversary of the *Titanic* disaster in 1914. Neither Lilian nor her brother married.

■ The *New York American* newspaper used many pages to describe the death of John Jacob Astor, one of the millionaires who drowned. However, the other 1,500 people who died were only mentioned in a few words at the bottom of the front page of the same newspaper.

Over 1,500 people died in the *Titanic* disaster, most of them sailors and male passengers. Among them were three extremely rich Americans – millionaires J. J. Astor, Isidor Straus, and Benjamin Guggenheim.

Captain Smith was among those who died. After the disaster, it was agreed that Captain Smith had been too confident, and not prepared for danger. A few years later, an international organization was started, so that ships would be better informed about icebergs. And after the *Titanic* disaster, all ships were ordered to carry enough lifeboats to save all the people on board.

5 Floods and storms

As we all know, water is absolutely necessary for life on Earth. Yet too much water in the wrong place can bring death and destruction. Floods have been part of human history for thousands of years. In recent centuries there have been extraordinary floods, especially in India, Bangladesh, China and the United States. There are two major causes of the floods in these countries: great rivers (for example, the Mississippi and the Ganges), and sea-storms whose tidal waves wash sea water all over the coast.

Bangladesh is a very low-lying country at the mouth of the River Ganges. It is one of the most highly-populated countries in the world, and many of its people live on land that is only centimetres above the level of the sea. Every year summer rains and the snow from the Himalaya mountains push the water-level up.

Floods in Bangladesh

■ In 1966, the beautiful town of Florence in Italy was hit by disastrous floods, which damaged or destroyed six million valuable books, thousands of old paintings, and hundreds of buildings. Some works of art were repaired with loving care, but many were lost for ever.

Florence after the floods

■ In China, the great Yellow River often floods. One story tells of a thirteen-year flood, 4,300 years ago. The Chinese Emperor (or King) asked Yu to control the floods, with great success. Yu later became the Emperor of China, and he is still remembered as 'Yu the Great'.

One of the worst flood disasters happened in November 1970, when a storm in the Bay of Bengal caused strong winds and waves at sea. These tidal waves made a moving wall of water, which then hit thousands of houses built on the low, flat land where the River Ganges meets the sea. Whole villages disappeared, and nearly one million people lost their lives.

At the time of this disaster, Bangladesh was called East Pakistan, and the central government of Pakistan was in Karachi, 2,400 kilometres away. Many people believed that the far-away government did not spend enough money to prevent and control floods. The 1970 flood helped to push East Pakistan towards self-government, and as a result the separate country of Bangladesh was born the following year.

In May 1985, another sea-storm hit Bangladesh, killing ten thousand poor farmers. By this time Bangladesh had good equipment for storm warnings. Warnings were sent to thousands of people who were living in villages near the coast, or on low-lying islands off the coast. One of these islands was called Urir Char, and many of the people had moved there after their homes were flooded and destroyed in the 1970 tidal wave. However, many of the poor farmers did not believe the warnings, and many did not want to leave their tiny pieces of land: all land in Bangladesh is valuable. Some people stood on the roofs of their houses, but they were washed away. Abu Qued survived by holding on to a tree, but his wife and six other people in his family were washed away by the water. Another man, Abdul Jalil, lost ten people from his family. His face was sad, but he could not cry: for him, as for many people in Bangladesh, this was simply the will of God.

In November 1977, a tidal wave six metres high hit the state of Andhra Pradesh, in India, causing ninety per cent of the people in some villages to lose their lives. For many days and weeks, the bodies of dead people and animals remained in the rivers.

In this flood, drowning was not the only cause of death. Floods often cut off roads, so food and medicines cannot reach the people near the disaster. In fact, as a result of the 1977 flood in Andhra Pradesh, one hundred thousand people died because they had no food to eat.

The United States also suffers from the destruction of wind and water. The mighty Mississippi is America's most important river, but it has always also been a great danger to life and land. For many years, the people who came to live near the Mississippi built great walls to hold back the waters after heavy rains.

However, in April 1927, the river broke through the walls, and the homes of 750,000 people disappeared under water. Millions of square kilometres of land in seven states were flooded. At one place, hundreds of people tried to reach safety by climbing on to a bridge. They stayed there for three days and three nights before people could save them.

■ In China, a great flood killed 900,000 people in September 1887. The Yellow River broke through walls and flooded eleven cities and 1,500 villages. In one place a dead child was found on a box, with food and its name attached – like a packet waiting to be found.

The Mississippi floods

> During the 1974 tornadoes, a nine-year-old boy was playing outside when the tornado picked him up, carried him 180 metres, and dropped him on the ground. His mother, his father, and his two sisters stayed at home and were killed.

A tornado

One small town was flooded with water seventeen metres deep, and the same nearly happened to the great city of New Orleans. However, the state government decided to make a hole in one of the flood walls, so that the brown flood-waters could find a shorter way to reach the sea. That hole saved the city, and many, many lives.

The great flood of April 1927 was not fully controlled until the month of July. By that time, 350,000 people were homeless, 300 people had died, and damage costing 300 million dollars had been caused.

After that disastrous flood, a new system of flood control was built along the Mississippi River. However, this did not prevent the river from flooding again in 1973 and 1983. In fact, a recent study has shown that the volume of water in the Mississippi has risen by 250 per cent in the last fifty years. It seems that there may be still more floods to come.

A tornado is a very, very strong wind that goes round and round in the shape of a tall, thin, chimney. In the centre of the tornado is a vacuum, which causes very high air pressure. The air in the centre goes round and round at a fantastic speed – the wind speed at the centre can be over 480 kilometres per hour.

Tornadoes are common in the Midwest of the USA, where they can cause great damage to buildings and injury to people. It is very difficult to know when a tornado is going to happen, and it is nearly impossible to make preparations before one arrives. They are one of the great forces of nature.

Over the years, tornadoes have caused death and damage in the Midwest of the USA, from the Gulf of Mexico north to Canada. They usually arrive between the months of March and July.

Disaster!

In just eight hours on 2nd and 3rd April 1974, about a hundred tornadoes killed 324 people in the American Midwest. Thousands of people were injured, and 400 million dollars of damage was caused to farms, homes, and buildings.

The worst-hit town was Xenia in the state of Ohio. In five minutes, the tornado left thirty people dead, 585 people injured, and thousands homeless. Half the town was destroyed. A lorry was blown into the sky, thrown into a tree, which then fell upside down, on top of the lorry! Packets of banknotes from a damaged bank building were found 300 kilometres away. All through the storm, an old woman sat in her chair after her house had blown way. She refused to move or to speak for many hours, because she simply could not accept that her house was no longer there.

■ Tornadoes make a huge noise when they arrive, but they normally only last for about fifteen minutes.

■ Between the years 1900 and 1969, some 12,000 people died in the USA because of tornadoes.

Texas: after a tornado

> ■ In the state of Alabama, the little town of Guin disappeared completely during the 1974 tornadoes. 'Guin just isn't there,' said one soldier. A radio reporter told his listeners, 'We can't talk to the police department. It just blew away.'

Although a tornado is an uncontrollable force of nature, its power is surprisingly exact. The great power is all held in the 'eye' or the centre of the tornado.

A man aged sixty-three in the state of Georgia pushed his wife and sons into the kitchen when the storm arrived. They were unhurt by the tornado. But the married daughter who lived next door was not so lucky. The daughter's house completely collapsed. The daughter and her son were dead, and the rest of her family lay dying or injured. The eye of the storm had passed directly over the daughter's house.

Similarly, one Xenia family found that their house had collapsed, except for one wall. Plates and dishes had been thrown into the washing machine, and pieces of wood had been pushed into the wall. But a box of soap powder stood untouched. The soap powder was just a few centimetres beyond the force of the tornado.

As happens with many disasters, people who are not involved seem to enjoy looking at the damage. In the state of Indiana, the National Guard had to use one thousand men to prevent sightseers from getting in the way of the emergency services. Every lorry in the state was needed to help to take food and water and medicines to the victims, but the sightseers got in the way.

6 Fire in Brazil

São Paulo is one of the largest cities in South America. In the mid-1970s, it had a population of about eight million people.

On 1st February 1974, the 650 workers at the Crefisu Bank went to work as usual, in their offices above a six-floor car park. But during the morning a fire broke out on the eleventh floor. The fire spread very quickly, and soon all the bank workers were trapped while the fire started to burn their hair and their clothes. Some people did not move: they just stood still, too frightened to move, and the flames ate them up.

Other people climbed up the stairs, higher and higher, trying to escape the killer-fire. But the smoke travelled

■ The temperature inside the Joelma building was so high that many of the bodies could not be recognized. This was why it took so long to count how many people died in the fire.

The bank burns

Rooftop rescue

- One of the worst fires ever happened in Chicago, USA, in 1903. The new Iroquois Theatre was very popular, but it was destroyed just six weeks after it opened, by a fire which killed over six hundred people.

- The Mayor of São Paulo promised that new building laws would be introduced. But the city did not have enough money or scientists to check and control the materials used for buildings, to make sure they would not catch fire easily. Safety is expensive.

- Firemen tried to stop people from jumping. They wrote a very big notice with the words, 'Courage, we are with you.' But most people panicked and jumped instead of waiting.

upwards too, followed by hot flames. Many people were unable to breathe, and the smoke probably killed them before their bodies were burned.

The heat of the fire prevented people from escaping downstairs to the ground floor, so many people decided to jump – but all those who jumped, jumped to their death. Others climbed on to the roof, and waited there to be rescued. Unfortunately, the firemen's ladders were too short to reach the roof; the people trapped there then had to choose between jumping and being burned alive. Many decided that a quick jump was better than a slow death by burning.

But there was one other possibility: rescue by helicopter. For two hours the fire was too hot for helicopters to land. So during those two hours, helicopters dropped boxes of milk to the people on the roof.

Some of the firemen did very dangerous things in order to save lives. Sergeant José Ruffino rescued eighteen people by holding on to a rope and then swinging across from another building to the burning bank. Each time he swung across, he caught and rescued one more person. Once he nearly fell to his death because a falling man hit him. But Ruffino managed to get back to safety. Later, after the flames had died down a little, the helicopters rescued nearly a hundred survivors from the roof.

In that disastrous fire, 227 people lost their lives. The cause is not known, but one thing is certain: the city's fire-fighting service was not good enough. São Paulo was the biggest city in Brazil at that time, but it had only thirteen fire stations, and it simply did not have the men and machines necessary to fight such a big fire. Another problem was that the building did not have enough fire escapes, so the people who were trapped inside had no way of reaching safety.

Disaster!

Another important aspect of this fire was the behaviour of many people in the city. Crowds and crowds of people watched from the streets nearby, fascinated by the horror before their eyes. For the sightseers it was perhaps like watching a horror film – live. But their interest had very serious results. Many fire engines could not reach the burning building, and ambulances could not take injured people to hospital because the roads were blocked. The fire was also shown on television, a decision which greatly angered the families of the dead and injured. Other people's interest in disasters is not always helpful.

■ The *Hindenburg* was a very successful airship travelling between Germany and the USA. Then on 3rd May 1937 it caught fire, killing thirty-three of the ninety-seven passengers.

The *Hindenburg in flames*

7 Bhopal, India

Bhopal is a city of nearly 700,000 people in the middle of India. The American chemical company, Union Carbide, has a large factory in Bhopal which makes chemicals for industry and for farmers. Some of the chemicals are used to make insecticides, which kill insects. Some of these chemicals are extremely dangerous.

One of the chemicals, methyl isocyanate, was kept in special containers under the ground. If the temperature was hotter than 38°C, the methyl isocyanate would become a deadly gas and it would escape into the air.

In November 1984, the special containers for the methyl isocyanate were being repaired. But at eleven o'clock on the night of 1st December, one of the factory workers noticed that the temperature of the methyl isocyanate was rising above 38°C. He and several other workers tried to bring the temperature down, but it was too late. Just before one o'clock in the morning of 2nd December, the deadly methyl isocyanate began to escape into the air.

■ When the chemical factory was opened again in order to make it safe, 200,000 people left the city. Bhopal was like a ghost town.

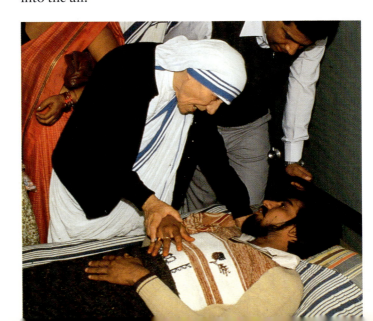

Mother Teresa visits Bhopal

Workers in the Union Carbide factory began to panic. Tears were in their eyes, and they could not breathe. The cloud of deadly gas began to move silently through the night air, passing over the poorer parts of the city. Hundreds of people died in their sleep. Poor people hoping to spend a warm night at the railway station continued to sleep, never to wake again. The station manager told a train driver not to stop at Bhopal. In this way he saved hundreds of lives before he himself died.

People living near the chemical factory thought that the end of the world had come – or perhaps it was a nuclear accident or an earthquake. Thousands tried to escape from the city. In cars, buses, by bicycle or on foot, they moved as fast as they could away from the city of death. Their eyes were crying, and many were blinded by the gas. They were weak and sick, and they could not breathe. Many started the journey but never finished. Some arrived, but then died a few hours later, after they thought they had reached safety.

By seven o'clock in the morning of 2nd December, 20,000 people had arrived at Hamidia hospital in Bhopal. But there were not enough medicines or doctors, and many people died while they were waiting. Mother Teresa of Calcutta came to visit and give comfort, but she could not bring the dying people back to health. The bodies of the dead were laid out in front of the hospital, waiting to be recognized by their families.

Many other people never reached the hospital. Dead bodies – both animals and people – lay all over the streets of the city. The wild dogs had plenty to eat during that time.

'I thought I had seen everything,' said a soldier in the Indian army, 'but this is worse than war.'

■ At Hamidia hospital in Bhopal, more than 350 doctors, 1,000 nurses and 500 medical students tried to help the victims of the poisonous gas.

The Union Carbide factory after the disaster

■ People who believe in the Hindu religion burn the bodies of the dead. So many people died at the time of the Bhopal disaster that huge fires burned all night long.

No-one knows exactly how many people died in the Bhopal disaster. The number of deaths was probably between 5,000 and 15,000, and at least 40,000 people were seriously injured. Many people went blind, and others always had problems with breathing. Mothers who had breathed the deadly methyl isocyanate gave birth to sick babies who died very quickly. Hundreds of people suffered many problems as a result of the disaster.

Who was to blame? The American head of Union Carbide flew to Bhopal a few days after the disaster. He was immediately arrested, but he was set free after six hours. Many people in India blamed the American company for the disaster – the American Union Carbide company owns 50.9 per cent of Union Carbide India. However, the question is not easy to answer.

The American company said that the safety system was the same for all Union Carbide factories – whether in India, the USA, Brazil, or anywhere else in the world. The only difference was the way the safety system was managed. The Indians, however, continued to blame the American company and tried to get money from them.

The lawyers no doubt made a lot of money out of the Bhopal accident. But all the money in the world can never bring back the people who died, or bring back the health of the survivors of the worst industrial accident in the world.

8 Chernobyl

Electricity is all around us – in thunder storms, in our bodies, in all things alive or dead. However, it is not easy to make and control electricity for us to use in our homes and in industry. Nuclear power is a way of making electricity that seems to be cheap and clean.

Chernobyl was a nuclear power station in the Ukraine (which used to be part of the old USSR). The power station in Chernobyl was made in a way that has not been accepted in other parts of the world. British scientists had looked at the design but decided that it was dangerous, because the reactor did not have enough protection in case anything went wrong.

In the middle of a nuclear power station are one or more reactors, which get extremely hot. If they get too hot, the reactors blow up.

■ After the Chernobyl disaster, many people told their governments that they did not want nuclear power. Although there have been changes as a result of Chernobyl, many people now believe that nuclear power will never be safe.

Chernobyl

28 — Disaster! —

■ Doctors believe that the Chernobyl disaster has caused at least 5,000 cancer deaths in Europe.

■ After Chernobyl, radioactivity in north-east Poland was 500 times the normal level. In parts of East Germany radioactivity was 100 times the normal level.

■ Marie Curie and her husband Pierre Curie discovered radium. In 1934 Marie Curie died of leukaemia, which is a sort of cancer. People think that her leukaemia was caused by radiation.

Very late at night on Friday 25th April 1986, some of the scientists at the Chernobyl power station decided to try a dangerous experiment. They changed the pressure in one reactor, which caused the temperature to rise. The reactor blew up.

Twenty people were working there at the time. One person was killed immediately, and his body has never been found. Several other people were killed soon after – some of them were fire-fighters who were helping to put out the fire. Other fire-fighters succeeded in putting out the fire before it reached the other three reactors at Chernobyl.

At first, the scientists and the government did not want to say that a really serious accident had happened. However, in the next days and weeks after the accident, the government of the Ukraine agreed that the air, food and water around Chernobyl were radioactive, and that it was dangerous for people to stay there. During the next few weeks, people in the city of Kiev, a hundred kilometres south of Chernobyl, wondered why there were no buses in their city! In fact, 1,200 buses from Kiev, and other towns, were being used to take people to a safer place. Later, 135,000 people were moved from around Chernobyl.

The rest of Europe first heard about the Chernobyl accident not from the USSR, but from Sweden, where radioactivity was noticed at the Forsmark nuclear power station. Denmark and Norway also reported an increase in radioactivity, and the scientists of western Europe finally realized that the radioactivity must be coming from near Kiev in the USSR.

The government of the USSR, however, said nothing to the world for two days after the accident. Because there was no hard information from the USSR, many wild stories began to be told, about thousands of deaths and cities living in fear. It was eighteen days before President Mikhail Gorbachev finally told the people of the USSR about the accident.

There is no doubt that the Chernobyl disaster was caused by human mistakes. The power station was not safe, and scientists at the power station were experimenting in dangerous ways. To make matters worse, the workers at the power station had no idea what to do in an emergency, and the government was extremely secretive.

The Chernobyl disaster had many effects on the electricity industry everywhere in the world. There had been nuclear accidents before, and many people had said for years that nuclear power was dangerous. This was the first really big accident that proved their warnings were right. Soon after the accident, many crowds of people met together in European cities. They held up notices with messages such as, 'Chernobyl is everywhere'.

Nuclear power was suddenly very unpopular, and governments had to look seriously for other ways of making electricity. That is why there is so much interest now in wind power and power from the heat of the sun.

■ On 28th March 1979, radiation at Three Mile Island in Pennsylvania, USA, was seventy-five times more than enough to kill one person. However, it seems that nobody was killed directly as a result of the accident.

Three Mile Island

9 The *Challenger* Disaster

During the 1950s, scientists from the USSR and the USA started a 'space race'. The first man to go into space was Yuri Gagarin, a Russian scientist who went round the Earth in 1961. Then in 1969, the American astronaut Neil Armstrong became the first person to walk on the Moon.

Since then many astronauts have travelled in space, and many children (and adults!) have dreamed of becoming an astronaut one day. For most people, this idea remains a dream, since only very experienced scientists can ever normally go into space.

In the 1980s, the USA began its space shuttle programme, which carries out many scientific experiments in space. The American government decided that the space shuttle called *Challenger* should take not only scientists, but also an ordinary person into space. This was a way of helping the American people to accept the great cost of the space shuttle programme.

In 1984, President Reagan of the USA decided that the 'ordinary' person should be a teacher. More than 11,000 teachers wanted the job, and the person who was finally chosen was Mrs Christa McAuliffe. While she was in space, she was going to give two fifteen-minute lessons by television, so that people all over the USA could understand the many advantages of space travel.

The scientists on board *Challenger* had many important jobs to do. *Challenger* was going to help other spacecraft to communicate with Earth. There were experiments which studied different types of light coming from Halley's comet, others which studied radiation in the spacecraft, and some which measured how heavy chicken eggs are in space!

The crew of the Challenger

Disaster!

Challenger had already been into space nine times before. This time, it was delayed, at first from 20 January 1986 to 25 January. Finally, on Tuesday 28 January, the shuttle was ready to go. The television cameras, the scientists, and the families of the astronauts were all in Florida, waiting to watch *Challenger* go off into space. Mrs McAuliffe's son Scott, aged nine, her daughter Caroline, aged six, her parents, and some of her students, were all there. This was a day that they would never forget!

The countdown started in long, slow minutes. Then, with forty-five seconds to go, things started to happen faster. The main engine was firing, the computers were in control. Ten ... nine ... eight ... seven ... six ... five ... four ... three ... two ... one ... lift off!

The Challenger *launch*

Disaster!

The explosion of Challenger

■ The *Challenger* disaster was the worst accident in twenty-five years of space travel. It was also the first time that American astronauts had been killed during a space flight.

Everybody's first feelings were pure joy and excitement. After fifty-two seconds, the engines had reached full power, and the shuttle was flying higher and higher up into space. A little later, an orange light was seen on the long-distance televisions, an unexpected light ... Then it was not just a small light, but red-and-orange fire, followed by a cloud of white smoke. Suddenly the televisions showed nothing, and all contact with *Challenger* was lost.

It was some time before anybody really accepted that a disaster had happened. Everybody wanted to believe that this was just a dream, that the shuttle and everyone inside would come back safely. But that was only a dream. The truth was hard to believe. *Challenger* had blown up in mid-air, seventy-three seconds after take-off. Mrs McAuliffe and the six other astronauts were dead.

Disaster!   33

Mrs McAuliffe had caught the imagination of the whole nation, because she represented every 'ordinary' person in America. Jay Schaeffer, a teacher from Los Angeles explained that for students, a teacher in space becomes their teacher: 'Do you know an astronaut? Everyone knows a teacher.' With her death, the American people lost confidence in the space programme.

In the next days, many nations of the world sent messages to President Reagan and to the families of the astronauts, expressing surprise and sadness. 'When something like this happens,' said a Russian woman in Moscow, 'we are neither Russians nor Americans. We all just feel sorry for those who died and for their families.'

A few weeks later, the bodies of the astronauts were found in the remains of the *Challenger* at the bottom of the Atlantic Ocean. The search cost twenty million dollars, but the nation could not rest until the bodies had been found.

The cause of the disaster was discovered quite quickly. At the time of the flight, the weather was freezing, and the cold had weakened the join between two parts of the shuttle. Fuel escaped, and this caused the fire and explosion.

The *Challenger* was not only a disaster for the families of Mrs McAuliffe and the six other astronauts. It was a disaster for the *Challenger* space programme, which had cost 1.2 billion dollars to develop. The scientists had hoped to learn a lot from the programme, so the disaster was a serious set-back for them. In future, the space programme would find it more difficult to get money from the US government.

However, the disaster could not completely stop the USA's space programme. As President Reagan said on television: 'There will be more shuttle flights ... more teachers in space. Nothing ends here. Our hope and our journeys continue.'

■ In 1971, three Russian astronauts returned to Earth after a successful twenty-four-day journey in space. However, when the door of the spaceship was opened, the three astronauts were found dead inside.

10 The *Exxon Valdez*

When we think of Alaska, most of us think of a far-away land in the frozen north-west of America. A land of clear sea and skies, and great natural beauty.

Alaska is also a land of great natural wealth. It has four great industries: fishing, forests, tourism and oil. On the south coast of Alaska is the port of Valdez, and from here most of Alaska's oil is taken to California and other parts of the USA.

On 24th March 1989, Captain Jeff Hazelwood was in command of an oil tanker which had the same name as the port of Valdez. The tanker was owned by the Exxon oil company, so it was usually called the *Exxon Valdez*. Captain Hazelwood was an experienced seaman who had loved the sea and sailing since he was a child. When he was thirty-two, he became the youngest man to take command of an Exxon oil tanker.

The Exxon Valdez

Disaster! | **35**

Although Captain Hazelwood was an excellent seaman, he had one major problem: he drank too much. In fact, at the time of the Valdez disaster, Captain Hazelwood was not allowed to drive a car because the police had caught him drunk while driving. However, Captain Hazelwood was still allowed to be in command of a ship.

The sea off the coast of Alaska is always dangerous because it is full of small islands and rocks, some of which lie hidden under the water. In winter and spring, there is another danger: ice.

The *Exxon Valdez* started its journey in the late evening of 24th March 1989. At first, Captain Hazelwood was controlling the ship. Later he went to his cabin to do some paperwork. He left the ship in the command of Third-Officer Cousins.

Just after midnight, the *Exxon Valdez* hit a group of rocks called Bligh Reef. The *Exxon Valdez* had five holes in its side – one of the holes was two metres wide by six metres long. Fifty million litres of oil started to flow out of the ship and into the sea. The captain sent a message: 'We're losing some oil and we're going to be here for a while.'

Unfortunately, the clean-up operation did not begin immediately. A special boat was supposed to be ready for emergencies, but it had been damaged by a storm. So the clean-up began fifteen hours after the oil-spill was first reported. The first two days after the spill had been calm and still; but by the time all the necessary equipment was in place, the weather had turned stormy. Strong winds quickly moved the oil to other parts of the sea, and the head of the Exxon oil company told newspaper and television reporters that the company had a real problem on its hands.

■ The birds and animals in Alaska suffered many different forms of death. Some froze to death because the oil prevented them from keeping warm. Others died because they ate birds covered in oil. And others died because they ate animals that had eaten birds covered in oil.

Disaster!

The clean-up operation for the Exxon Valdez cost 2.5 billion dollars.

Disaster!

The oil from the Valdez disaster polluted nearly 1,700 kilometres of Alaska's coast, and it covered 4,800 square kilometres of water. It was the worst oil-spill in American history. Millions of fish, 300,000 sea birds, and thousands of sea-otters died. The bodies of sixteen whales were found. Some animals and birds died from cold, others died from hunger, since twenty-five per cent of the plankton of the sea were destroyed in the disaster. Plankton are tiny, tiny little plants and animals which live in the sea and which are a very important part of the food chain: plankton are eaten by small fish, which are eaten by bigger fish, and so on ...

■ Between 1991 and 1994, several studies showed that the cost and the environmental problems of the clean-up were greater than the problems caused by leaving the oil in the sea.

It is easy to try to blame one person for the *Exxon Valdez* disaster. In fact, the disaster was the result of mistakes made by many different people: people in the Exxon oil company, people on land, and people on the tanker. Perhaps the greatest mistake was the view of people in the oil industry who said, 'There has never been a disaster, so a disaster will never happen.' We call this view complacency.

■ Oscar the sea-otter has lived among the fishing boats of Valdez town for five years. The fishermen and tourists give him food, and he enjoys his dinner of fish with other sick otters.

The *Exxon Valdez* disaster had a great effect on the oil industry. Every nation uses energy for transport and industry, and to make electricity. That energy must come from somewhere – from the sun, wind, water, oil, gas, or nuclear power. The need for cheap energy means that oil companies are always trying to keep costs down. This often means that fewer people work longer hours, and they may therefore not work so well. This leads to the possibility of serious accidents.

A sea-otter

11 The Kobe Earthquake

■ In 1906, the city of San Francisco was shaken by an earthquake. It only lasted 48 seconds, but it caused millions of dollars of damage, and it killed 3,000 people.

Japan has always had earthquakes. Many Japanese homes are built in a special way, so that they can better survive earthquakes. Many Japanese people are ready with different ways of surviving an earthquake. Some Japanese children also enjoy earthquake computer games, which give them the feeling of what a real earthquake might be like!

There was a very big earthquake in Tokyo on 1st September 1923, which killed 143,000 people. Japanese people still remember 1st September as National Disaster Prevention Day. However, neither the memory of 1923 nor all the earthquake preparations seemed to help the people of Kobe, in south Japan, when an earthquake hit their city on 17th January 1995.

At 5.45 a.m. on that Tuesday, when many people were still asleep, the ground began to shake. Roofs fell in, roads suddenly disappeared, cars and houses collapsed. An earthquake measuring 7.2 on the Richter scale had hit the city.

The destruction was unbelievable. One train station collapsed, destroying many cars in its car-park. A motorway simply fell down to one side. The lines of the 'bullet train' broke in eight places.

In total, about 310,000 people – one fifth of the city's population – were without homes, 6,440 buildings collapsed, and more than 5,000 people were killed.

Japanese children on an earthquake exercise

Disaster!

The Kobe earthquake measured 7.2 on the Richter scale. The 1906 earthquake in San Francisco, USA, was thirty times stronger than the 1995 Kobe earthquake.

40 — *Disaster!* —

- In 1755, there was a terrible earthquake in the city of Lisbon, Portugal. After the earthquake, the city was completely destroyed by a fire which lasted for nine days and nine nights. Then a great wave came in from the sea, and many people were drowned. About 60,000 people were killed in the disaster.

There were many problems for the survivors and the rescuers. Many parts of the city had no water, either for drinking or for washing. Many roads were destroyed, so it was impossible at first to take food, water and medicine to injured people. And the weather was cold!

Although people were freezing with cold in some places, there were unwanted fires in other places. In fact, fire moved through many parts of the city, and caused as much destruction as the actual earthquake.

There were many sad stories of death and loneliness. People heard the voice of a little girl calling for her mother under the remains of their house, 'Okasan, okasan,' 'Mother, mother.' But the calling stopped at seven o'clock in the evening: the rescuers did not arrive in time. Nearby, a statue of Kannon, the female Buddha, stood among the collapsed buildings. Her name means 'the person who hears cries.'

- The worst earthquake disaster in the twentieth century was the 1976 Tangshan earthquake in China, which killed more than 250,000 people.

About one hour after the earthquake, one man was standing at a bus-stop, waiting for a bus to go to work. Perhaps he was hoping that if he did a normal day's work, then life would return to normal. But the bus never arrived.

One old man sat in front of his collapsed house and drank Japanese wine. 'What can you do except drink sake and smile?' he said.

In the late twentieth century, the Japanese people had started to believe that scientists could always warn them when an earthquake was going to hit Japan. People also felt that, after the experience of so many earthquakes, they were better prepared for such a disaster.

- One of the worst earthquakes in the world happened in Shanxi, China, in 1556. It is thought that 830,000 people died – nine times more people than in the worst volcanic eruption.

In fact, it seems that scientists can never fully protect people from earthquakes and their destruction. No one can be complacent about the force of nature.

12 Conclusion

People's reactions to disasters are very different. Some panic and behave wildly, in ways which are quite unintelligent. Others pretend that the disaster is not happening, and they behave as if everything is normal. Others show great self-control, and they are probably the people who are most helpful in the middle of disaster.

After disasters, many people give money to help the victims. Some people may want to spend the money on making changes to prevent new disasters. Others may want to spend the money on things to help them remember the dead – or even on prizes for the rescuers.

One of the clearest lessons to be learned from disasters is the danger of complacency. It is so easy to think that a disaster will not happen because it has not yet happened. This was one of the problems with the *Exxon Valdez*.

Disasters also show us how dangerous science and scientific experiments may be. At Bhopal the scientists were not careful enough, and at Chernobyl they were doing a dangerous experiment. People were complacent about the dangers that they were playing with.

Environmental disasters, such as Chernobyl and the *Exxon Valdez* raise the question of how we find the energy and power that we need. As a result of those disasters, governments and scientists have started to think seriously about finding different types of energy. Those disasters caused great damage to the environment, but they were a turning-point in people's opinions about the energy industry and the environment.

Natural disasters, such as earthquakes, tornadoes and volcanoes will always be a danger for people living in certain parts of the world. Warnings can be given, preparations can be made, but we cannot be completely protected from the full force of nature.

Exercises

A Checking your understanding

Write answers to these questions from Chapters 1–3.
1 What are the two main causes of disasters?
2 What are the names of the two towns which were destroyed by the eruption of Vesuvius in A.D.79?
3 Why is the eruption of Vesuvius in A.D.79 so important for us today?
4 How did the Great Fire of London start?
5 Why was King Charles popular at the time of the Great Fire of London?

Write answers to these questions from Chapters 4–6.
1 Why did the *Titanic* sink?
2 How do we know that Lilian Asplund never got over her experience of the disaster?
3 How did the 1970 flood help to push East Pakistan towards self-government, and what is the name of the new country?
4 What is a tornado?
5 How would you describe Sergeant José Ruffino?

Write answers to these questions from Chapters 7–9.
1 Why did the deadly chemical, methyl isocyanate, escape into the air?
2 Why were thousands of people moved from around Chernobyl after the accident?
3 Name the two most important causes of the Chernobyl nuclear accident.
4 Why do you think the government of the USSR said nothing about the Chernobyl accident for two days?
5 Why did Mrs Christa McAuliffe go into space?
6 What caused the *Challenger* disaster?

Write answers to these questions from Chapters 10–12.
1 What do you think of when you think of Alaska?
2 How many kilometres of Alaska's coast were polluted by the *Exxon Valdez* oil-spill?
3 Which words in the text explain the meaning of 'complacency'?
4 Why was 1st September chosen as National Disaster Prevention Day in Japan?

Disaster! — 43

5 What sort of problems did the Kobe earthquake cause for the survivors and rescuers?
6 Explain three different ways that people behave in a disaster.

B Working with language

1 _Put the sentences of this summary of the Chernobyl disaster in the right order._
Then join the parts together to make four sentences with correct capital letters
and punctuation.
1 ... scientists in Chernobyl tried a dangerous experiment ...
2 the rest of Europe heard about the Chernobyl accident ...
3 because the air, food and water there were radioactive ...
4 ... when nuclear power stations in Denmark and Norway reported an increase in radioactivity ...
5 ... in the weeks and months after the accident, the government of the Ukraine sent 135,000 people away from around Chernobyl ...
6 ... which made the temperature of one reactor rise ...
7 ... coming from near the city of Kiev in the USSR ...
8 ... there is now much more interest in other ways of making electricity ...
9 ... so it blew up ...
10 ... as a result of the Chernobyl nuclear disaster ...

2 _Use these words to join two sentences together. They all come from the story of_
the Titanic.
but so that when so
1 It was spring-time ...
2 Before the journey, her father had had a bad dream about the idea ...
3 Edith, her mother and the other survivors saw a sea full of bodies and icebergs ...
4 The Captain went to see the hole and saw water entering the ship ...
5 A few years later, an international organization was started ...

a ... Captain Smith knew there might be ice in the sea
b ... her mother had decided that they must go
c ... he immediately ordered the lifeboats
d ... ships would be better informed about icebergs
e ... the sun rose the next morning

44 —————————————— *Disaster!* ——————————————

3 *Choose the best linking word and complete these sentences with information from the story about the Kobe earthquake.*
1 Japanese people remember 1st September *because/so/that* ...
2 It was impossible to take food, water and medicine to injured people *because/although* ...
3 The man at the bus-stop probably thought that *when/if* he did a normal day's work ...
4 Many Japanese people had started to believe that scientists could prepare them for any earthquake *but/and* ...

C Activities

1 Write a letter to a friend describing the panic and the rescue work during the fire disaster in São Paulo, Brazil.
2 You are a television reporter. Write a list of questions that you will ask when you interview Captain Hazelwood a few days after the *Exxon Valdez* disaster.
3 Explain to your friends (in writing or in speech) why Mrs Christa McAuliffe went into space, and what happened.

D Project work

1 In groups, discuss ways in which you would make plans in case of: (a) an earthquake (b) a flood (c) a volcano.
2 Imagine that a group of you are on the last voyage of the *Titanic*. One of you is Captain Smith, one of you is the look-out boy, one of you sends radio messages. The others are rich passengers, poor passengers, and ordinary sailors. Prepare the conversation in different situations:
(a) the Captain at the controls/at a dinner party, (b) the look-out boy when he sees the iceberg, (c) the rich passengers dancing and singing, (d) the poor passengers down below, (e) the final panic.

Then act out the last hours before the *Titanic* sank to the bottom of the Atlantic.

Glossary

archaeologist a person who studies things from history

ash grey powder which remains after a fire

astronaut a person who travels into space (e.g. to the Moon)

brandy a very strong (alcoholic) drink

bullet train a very fast train (in Japan)

cargo the things which a ship carries

chemical a special powder or liquid which is used for science or medicine

collapse to fall down and break up completely

destruction destroying, making something into nothing

drown to go under water and die

earthquake a sudden movement of the earth

energy force or power which makes things change, work, or happen

environment the natural world around us

erupt to blow up (e.g. a volcano)

experiment a test to try new ideas; scientists do experiments

factory a place where things are made

fascinate to interest very much

female of a woman, not of a man

flood too much water on land (from a river or the sea)

force power which makes things move or work

fuel something which makes machines work, e.g. oil, gas

government the people who control a country

industry making things in a factory

luxury expensive things which make life very comfortable

mayor the most important person in control of a city

merchant a person who buys and sells things

motorway a very fast road

mud wet earth

nuclear from part of an atom; nuclear power can give us electricity

panic the feeling that you do not know what to do, e.g. after an accident

pepper a powder which makes food taste hot

Disaster!

pollute to make something dirty (e.g. the air or a river)

port the place where a ship leaves land, or arrives back to land

power force, energy, which makes things move or work

pressure pushing very, very hard

programme plan

radiation dangerous heat (e.g. from nuclear power)

radioactive sending out dangerous heat

rat a big mouse, which may cause disease

reaction people's thoughts and feelings after something has happened

reactor part of a nuclear power station (which makes electricity)

rescue to save

Richter Scale a measure of how strong an earthquake is

scientist a person who studies science

sink to go down into water

space the sky, the Moon, the Sun and beyond

spill (liquid) to go over the top of something, or through a hole

swing to go through the air

tanker a big ship which carries oil

tidal caused by tides, which pull the sea backwards and forwards

vacuum an empty space, with no air in it

volcano a mountain which blows up with fire

whale a very big animal (not a fish), which lives in the sea